A lens in the palm

Kelly Grovier was born in Grand Rapids, Michigan. He is a lecturer in English and Creative Writing at Aberystwyth University. *A lens in the palm* is his first collection of poems.

KELLY GROVIER

A lens in the palm

Oxford*Poets*

CARCANET

First published in Great Britain in 2008 by
Carcanet Press Limited
Alliance House
Cross Street
Manchester M2 7AQ

A CIP catalogue record for this book is available from the British Library
ISBN 978 1 903039 88 5

The publisher acknowledges financial assistance from Arts Council England

Typeset by XL Publishing Services, Tiverton
Printed and bound in England by SRP Ltd, Exeter

for Sinéad

Acknowledgements

I am grateful to the editors of the following publications where versions of some of these poems appeared for the first time: *Oxford Magazine*, OxfordPoets 2004 (Carcanet), *New Welsh Review*, *Planet*, *poems.com*, *Poetry London*, *Poetry Review*, *Poetry Wales*, *PN Review*, *Stand*, and *Quadrant*.

Warm thanks are also due to David Constantine, Bernard O'Donoghue, and to my friends and colleagues in Oxford and Aberystwyth without whom these poems would not have been written.

Contents

The lens	11
Moons	12
The Consolation of Philosophy	13
Ghosting	14
The stars	15
Conversions: the ruined statue of a saint	16
Furcula	17
The frequency	18
There	19
The recipe	20
The line	21
Gumbo	22
What the ceiling said	23
Mincing words	24
Of thought – the train	25
Midas	26
Rodin's *Balzac*	27
The ancient of days	28
Hierakonpolis	29
Extraction	30
The ledger	31
Not amnesia	32
'Nor even yet quite relinquish –'	33
The shed	34
Tens and eight	35
Via negativa	36
Between stations	37
Les Parapluies	38
Rain, Steam, and Speed	39
The easel of Mantegna	40
A spider in Trinity College chapel	41
Reflections on a steel teapot	42
In the National Library of Ireland	43
The triple tree	44
Metaphysics	45
The six fifteen	46
Camping out	47

Spinnings	48
Strange currencies	49
Shutters	50
The ghost grove	51
Tractatus	52
The things of snow	53
Working some things through	54
The metal clasp	55
The night is like a dinosaur	56
Giotto	57
April morning	58
Flickering out	59
A suite of bats	60
Landscape with coffee and wings	64
Philosophy of language	65
Sight, unseen	66
Lacewing	67
Palms	68

Something strange is the soul on the earth ...
Georg Trakl

The lens

Tonight, the stars are suffering
from a tinnitus
                    pitched so high

not even the slightest
                            icicle shatters

and the ringing triggers
                            a forgetfulness
in the trees
                who've draped themselves
in thin
            nightgowns of snow.

In this heartbreaking stillness
                            a holly-
bush brings to focus
                        a lens in the palm

of its serrated hand
                        and the whole world

ceases to exist.

Moons

We reach this place
through a gauze of snow
and lamplight, our faces

frozen useless as language
and the windows bracketing
a fur of candles, binding us

in a glaze of hesitations:
a woman, sitting at a kitchen
table, arranging her soul

into angles, measuring
a space in which we matter,
not to ourselves, but to those

whose lips are trapped
like ours, in a furze
of moonness and ice.

The Consolation of Philosophy

It wasn't that we weren't there
to appreciate it in all its splendour
when the snow fell on the mountain
blossoming in a mind
that had long since vanished; we were
there but didn't know
what to look for. The words our eyes

drank from weren't about snow
or mountains but about the complexities
of a relationship that the poet
imagined in the shadow of snow
meshing a distance in which
the mountain was only discernible
in flashes: not so much reading

between the lines as seeing the lines
in the context of the snow,
the snow in the context of the mind
in the context of the mountain
which imagines a distant blossoming
of eyes: April, and the complexities
of the landscape aren't at all

like those faced by Boethius, only
the suggestion of flowers suggesting
what's lost when love is lost
and the satisfying crunch of frost
underfoot – like a threshold,
bringing the awkward mountain
that much nearer.

Ghosting

There are reasons to suppose
we may be ghosted
by what we touch: the clipped-

fin carp, prisming
our existence, the kingfisher, scarfed
in mist, refracting

murmurs – each encoded replication
dissolving what we
might have been in another

world: lips of rain
pursing from the edge of a crocus
petal, light reckoning

from a font, shudders of unbeing
in which we're fleshed
with absence, souled in luminous dust.

The stars

think themselves into existence
and know themselves too good
for words:

dippers,

plough.

The trouble comes at picnics –
the last to leave, lovers lying
head to head, sky-faced,

naming the unnameable with eyes
closed – flickerings – the unknown
knowing the unknowable. After a while,

it becomes difficult to separate
what about them moves the most –
the bright intangibility of something

that's no longer there from the utter
absence that beckons in between –
the echoed darkness or the dark

unechoing. 'Look,' she says,
pointing to neither,
'how cold is that?'

Conversions: the ruined statue of a saint

His face is all fucked-up from frost,
   scarred by slackening sun;
two fingers that were raised to Christ
   have webbed themselves to one;

the long lithe line that sealed the lips
   has slowly weathered wide;
a sense of sway down robe-hung hips
   has smoothed into his side –

swimming, beneath a million skies –
   estranged, amphibian –
till all is changed, even the eyes,
   back into God again.

Furcula

for my father

By the time the guests had gone,
there was little left to save still clinging
to the carcass – only a slush

of grease and the slender wish-
bone, unbroken. Tipsy, I propped
its antlers up like a cockeyed

crucifix in the kitchen window,
to see the moon thin and the stars
pin themselves along the unanswerable

axis of its perpetuating Y – like a twig
in the palms of the infinite, dowsing
for our inscrutable blood. In the morning,

I watched a pigeon pause
along the ledge, looking in, nodding
to himself, knowing

that what he saw pointed in
two directions: towards everything,
towards absolutely nothing at all.

The frequency

The radio and the inconceivable
distance of a tragedy
taking place somewhere –

the movement of a satellite
this way or that in the vast
torso of an atmosphere – the tiny

spindles of copper thread
that lead to the adjustment
of the small serrated dial calibrated

to keep the suffering low –
the button of the synchronised
SNOOZE. Drowsy, I let that

sink in and flip over to hear
a sharp scrawny cry coming
from a pink panache above

snow, clinging to a cherry
blossom like a feeling, wanting
to be close, to be near me.

There

We were there – weren't we? –
when the sun filled itself
with milk, shallowing the last

footprints of the moon –
and the wallpaper *I must remember
to mention the wallpaper*

was doilied with the silhouettes
of bougainvillaea sprigs
against a field of darkness;

a stranger was waiting in the light
while at our feet
cockroaches rustled like my mother's

hands – he was waiting and I
forgot to misprize him
of each place he'd followed us to,

keeping scraps of shadows –
filling himself with what we were.
Yes, come to think of it, between

the two of us, I'm almost
certain now that I, I
was the one was there.

The recipe

calls for thirty years of fear;
chin trembles in an empty street
for no apparent reason; it calls
for sweating when someone
makes reference to you-know-
what, and a short sharp needle
jab in the side of your neck whenever

the phone rings. A train
rumbles past and its freight doors
are open facing you; you recognise
the cargo as it passes by one car
at a time: father, mother, brother,
son. When the rain begins, you try
to separate its strands like a bead

curtain, but start slipping on the glass
sliding under your feet. At first,
your calves hurt, and your thighs,
but after awhile you forget about
the pain and spend your time
trying to remember what it was
the recipe called for next.

The line

At first, they sat on the line,
drooping between farms,
like a row of birds perched
on a wire. Every once in a while,
one would flap its syllables,

batting the sun back, making us
blink. It was always November.
When a new one landed,
the strand shook like the sea,
and for a moment the world

would mean something different.
When autumn finally arrived,
and I came out to greet you,
we stared at the empty cord,
slung across the sky, waiting

for one to swoop down,
wondering why the wire was
grinning back at us – wondering
where it was our lives
had disappeared to.

Gumbo

for my mother

Clay–skyed, weatherless;
I find myself in the days
before the levees' slack,

souping in the rich hand-
me–down recipes of voodoo
and jazz – cardinals, sharding

round the pecan trees
and the air, bouillabaisse.
On Tchoupitoulas Street,

we scrounged for lady-
fingers to knuckle into rue
and dusted ourselves down

with beignets when a pair
of blue–tinged biddies
cut across us puckering

at the haze saying, 'Weather's
not good, is it?' 'No,
but better than nuthin.'

What the ceiling said

How long have we been
lying here, scrunched up
on a single mattress, the humid

rhythms of your breath
lulling my nightmares to sleep?
In this brief interstice

between consciousness, the patch
of white above our bodies
has started to stir. Cherubim

surface briefly, then recede.
My mother's face. A magpie.
And that thing I never told you.

Suddenly, a sense of words
merges with the grinding of teeth
and I find myself shushing you

half-awake, straining with both
my ears to hear what it is
the ceiling is trying to tell me.

Mincing words

On an open green
in Alton, sweet
Fanny Adams was cut

to pieces. Soldiers sod-
dened in the trench
joked the meat they ate

was sweet Fanny A-
dams. Sweet Fan-
ny Adams, cut to pie-

ces on an open green
in Alton – a name in-
terred into our exp-

letives as unutt-
erable – a sign scar-
red with asterisks

stigmatised like skin
stamped upon
with meaning: *f*** all.*

Of thought – the train

Just beyond the dust-
and mud-spackled pane,
beyond the slurried

margin of stagnant slip-
stream shadowing the track,
and the sleet-pocked swathe

of straggling crabgrass,
where magpies bullyboy
the bluetits and beer cans

hunk with glint, a make-
shift bridge lobs itself over
the awkward Ystwyth,

sheep clump in clots of mist
and the earth slides slowly
backwards up into something

like a mountain – its gold-
and-green-stippled sides,
gorse-glutted, gangle past

hummocks of heather
and shattered cairns
to a stammering eminence,

wipe their forehead
on a handkerchief of wind,
and *phew*, back to the train,

its knots dissolving, one by
one like gutturals,
into a throat of trees.

Midas

for Damian Walford Davies

When the pickaxe prized
the tomb of Midas,
fingers froze from the funk

of odours, lasers licked
the leather and scrapings scanned
revealed ravishings, remains

of a lamb, and resin in a sacra-
mental skull, divulged the nature
of the ritual that cured his body

for a second birth – the balms
of blood, the lacerated birds –
and the myth, through thirty

centuries' must, into the air
like a vapouring frost.
So tell me, fat man,

with your mouth of mould,
what happened when you touched
the hand of God?

Rodin's Balzac

When he comes to you,
like a glacier of bruised
bronze, wedging his way

through your mind, shifting
his weight, neither forward
nor back, but upon some hidden

human knowledge, the sunken
sockets will not seem like eyes
unformed – two abysses

where the thumbs stuffed
the isolation and the loneliness
and the incomprehensible

despair – but dark lamps shining
in the nothingness, the huge
abdomen will not seem

obscene, stomaching the absence
like an ocean, angling
under unundulating skies.

The ancient of days

That summer, I was the broken
clock on the old church tower
in the little village square. Pigeons
would gather beneath me
and I would mark the passage
of time by the length
of their shadows, the rhythm

of their ritual dance. With teeth
clenched and hands
frozen on the hour of a death –
unable to relinquish
even a minute – I compassed
silently in the air, arranging
the universe into angles, calibrating

the wavelength of stars, while
behind me, on the other side
of the wall, with his arms stretched-
out straight for eternity, staring
at an empty cup, there was
another, who was hell-
bent, trying to disprove me.

Hierakonpolis

for Jem Poster

Beneath the living tissue of the living
sky, the limestone has an air
of consciousness about it, the air

a quality of bone. Here, where no one
will ever feel to find us – our limbs
linened in resin and throats clipped

in honour of Osiris – we keep quiet,
of necessity, our reflection is eternal,
our grief, and we scale ourselves

in amulets of tears – gold and gauzy
green – an atmosphere of earth
setting above us, and every now

and then the heart-beat sound vibrating
hooves make, against the wind-
veined level, the soul-inhuming sky.

Extraction

Bent-necked, staring over
the lip, the lamp's fluorescence
is a close horizon just beyond

the deviated-septum rise of fore-
shortened freckles and my posture
is incongruously relaxed to suffer

the needle prick prophylactic
fingers bring. Phobic, fidgety,
I feel a sharp pang knowing

that this sonata is something
I will never be able to listen to again
with pleasure, as stolidity seeps

into my cheek. Suddenly, I am
the poet in the *Fall of Hyperion*,
mounting steps to Moneta's

throne – my face half-flesh-half-
stone – my tongue now undecided
about the possibility of speech as it

lies like a stricken serpent in its
cave: *an' wheh I cloath my eyeth,
fwighthened a' the thight of forthepth,*

*ath the thound of cwunthing bown
beginth, aul I can think uf ith haw
ahpwohpweeit my pwayrs muth soun*

*to Goth, whooth own voith in the thark
flowethenthlethneth uf Nathur ith nuffing
buh infwecthed nummneth, mumbled thounds.*

The ledger

in which you record the names
of those responsible. Your great-
grandfather, whose blurred

black-and-white face got warped
by rain when the glass cracked.
The uncle with the one arm,

and the niece who died in child-
birth everyone always said looked
just like you. A pluck of a string

like music to a spider's ear who knows
by the merest vibration of floss
which quadrant of his spun harp

a thing has come to die in. Beyond
the webbed window, a fawn
inspects her spots in the pale light

of the full moon and your mind
becomes your fingers fumbling
with something folded in your

pocket. A prescription you never
returned for. The name is yours,
and the signature, but you don't

recognise the writing as you begin
copying each syllable
onto the next line of the ledger.

Not amnesia

From daily occurrences.
Long strings of numbers.
Birth dates. Or your mother's.

Maiden name. And not.
From the way that people.
Look. Not from. Who you are.

A shadow. That pauses before.
Deciding to walk in the opposite.
Direction. A mirror that stops.

Pretending. A tree that can't.
Remember its leaves.
Or the sky. Where all the stars go.

'Nor even yet quite relinquish –'

There are ways of lingering here.
The trick is to locate the place
where the inside and the outside

cling – the membrane of equilibrium
where sky and consciousness are
held in abeyance, in balance, being

neither sky nor consciousness. No
wonder so many have searched for it
in eyes – 'two jellied tears filled

with arrogance and pride and fore-
knowledge of death' – but even eyes
participate too much in one side

or the other, depending on who's be-
holding and who is being held.
Paracelsus said, 'No thing heavy can be

made light without help from the light
thing.' Or else he should have.
How come you never look at me?

The shed

Tonight, the moon is a voice
disguising a language
you once found familiar

and your hands have that strange
look words sometimes get
when looked at too long.

Suddenly, a shed door swings
open and the whirr of a drill
draws you in. Oak shards scrape

bright scratches in the air
then disappear like fireflies.
'Death is a joiner,' you say

to yourself, staring at the tools,
while all around the rain
rattles on the roof and the wind,

like a breathing –
or that thing that comes,
just after breathing.

Tens and eight

We were tens and eight, my brother,
the dead boy, and I. An August
sleepover, backyard pup-tents
and kerosened silhouettes of finger-bats
and cluck-knuckles, and in the morning
snuck out on our goose-necks
for Calabazas Creek, the squidge

of tadpoles burping around
beer cans and the rusted ribs of a ditched
trolley. It was they who shared
freckles, he and Danny, like a secret
language as we skimmed bottle tops
off the greasy swill, flicking dog-ends
and grotty screws, squinting in the grubbed

heat as I nudged a comma of sweet sap
from a filched waffle with my sun-burnt
tongue. What I want to say is that, looking
back, I saw it coming in the light shuddering
off the mottled water, or that there was
something in the way his body blinked
in the haze as we skittled for our bikes

that signalled he was going or was already
gone; that what we saw crumple between
fender and gravel was something other
than everything, that even now there are
ways of shifting your focus from the ruined
faces round that wreck, deciphering
freckles, distinguishing shoes.

Via negativa

for Kevin Mills

Always to think,
to suffer the abiding
disregard of a universe

of feeling:
the trees about you
don't care,

and the landscape owns
no guilt: O,
to live in a world

in which the small things
alter and die –
and even the eternal.

Between stations

where *here* is neither is
nor *there* more
than superstition. Outside,

I can feel the fields'
respiring mist nuzzling
into frost and in the merging

darkness we listen
for something trapped
between thinking

and enunciation,
pursing its soft
invisible lips: *shhh*.

Les Parapluies

for Anthony Mosawi

X-rays of the Renoir
and the breaking
of the frame, the stretching

over of the canvas
and a horse hair frozen
in gesso like a fracture

in the skull. Outside,
crowds are gathering in heavy
overcoats for the late

opening hours of the exhibition,
and there's an iridescence
hanging in the distance –

a pigeon frumping up
to where Lord
Nelson holds the deep

blue-umbrellaed sky
above us – the stars,
just beginning to fall.

Rain, Steam, and Speed

Attention was then squarely
focused on the train – how its engine
emerged from fire coagulating

around the curve. Then my focus
shifted – I grew tall enough
to find the hare in front – the machine

retreating to mirage behind it.
Now my mind returns to the hazy
margins left of the track:

were those angels scumbling
in the water? Was that water? My eyes
seem less and less instrumental

than they were – my mind,
like a canvas tilting – the air clumped
with oil, still waiting to be squeezed.

The easel of Mantegna

Empty-armed, like a soldier,
waiting for the deposition
still to happen, watching

as the rough skin is stretched
across the squat square ribs
and stapled, scraped

with a palette knife, before
the morbid undertaking
of the gesso and the paint.

Or say instead you always
were inclined to play
an active role in this,

our cruellest fiction: empty-
angled and pristine save
where you were brushed

with the death and cleansed
with the dizzy stench of spirit.
You are the awkward ladder,

the hallowed steps, the endless
air forever drifting through
the thin rafters of an unroofed

steeple – on or in or out of
whom the wide sound
of resurrection still remains

for us a thing we listen for
in silence:
untolled, unrunged.

A spider in Trinity College chapel

Tiny abseiler, dangling
from the marble index
finger of Sir Isaac Newton,

how many hands meditate
the hours of this, your dust–
bejewelled dial? The evening sun,

spinning through the mullioned
mosaic of medieval
glass above you, glistens

on the unglazed angles
of your fragile rose window,
as if the air itself were being

sewn together and time
were nothing more than silk
quilts God used to bind

the struggling souls
on whom he comes
to prey.

Reflections on a steel teapot

Great Distorter of Truth,
you who would exaggerate
the size of the sugar bowl

and flip my reflection up-
side-down, why so pouty,
Mr Elbow-bent Hand-on-

hips? Have all the leaves
inside you grown
so bitter and so cold?

In the National Library of Ireland

Rummaging through the dimly-lit
cabinets of the Retrospective, our eyes
thumb past weathered letters and rusted

specs and reach at last a lung of lapis
lazuli. The two Chinamen are here, frozen
in speech, and the lagging servant lugging

scrolls, lulled forever by the polished
music of that rippling stone. In the glass's
glare, we clock behind us the ebb

and flow of visitors gauzing off
to other galleries as our breaths blur
into its sculpted blue, searching

in veins for that one detail we never
found – the fiery feathers of the long-
legged bird that carried our souls away.

The triple tree

We could say it was winter,
or you could ask
what the hangman was doing

spinning loops of gold
by the glass gallows.
Either way, we found

ourselves, eyes smeared
with darkness, the moon,
measuring wrists, sweeping

the scaffold, raising cross-
beams of ice. The hurdle.
A slipknot of stars.

Metaphysics

Amid all this talk of the unknown,
the incomprehensible,
what's increasingly difficult to prove

is the really obvious about us.
Across the street, pale light
comprehends a cherry blossom

that yesterday wasn't there
and I saw ringlets of pink paint
peeling off an empty house

somewhere in my childhood.
I know the connection
between the two is something

altogether clear – something
I will spend my whole life
trying to create.

The six fifteen

So there he sat, flipping
coins, waiting for it
to end. But the day refused
to break. Never mind

the mice inhabiting his shirt,
or the snow falling
in his slippers. His freckles
pointed to a brouhaha

in his future. Something
in his past. Over that ruddy
constellation he stared at me,
as if the sheer distances

I'd wandered, the mystics
groomed and dark cathedrals
plundered, qualified me
to poke him in the shoulder

with a broken stick or to read
the bus schedule in an ancient
tongue. Without an accent.
To give him change.

Camping out

The infinite regression of things
was never made clearer to you
than that starless night
when you took the form
of a chattering chicken's head
projected onto the nylon
wall of a tent, and looking back

at the pinched forefinger and thumb
that made your beak, back
through the clenched middle and ring
fingers to the flickering
kerosene lantern, you knew that even he,
your pudgy, rotten-toothed, dim-
witted creator, could not behold what

you, a knuckle-brained silhouette
could see on the other side
of the screen: the racoon at the picnic
basket, the speckled fawn disappearing
under brush for fear, and beyond
the timberline, the fat orange moon
that was busy, obliterating the stars.

Spinnings

We've come this way before –
haven't we? – the lanes wet, deepening
the burgundy squelch

of leaves, and the hedges plotting
an articulate sky.
It's all much closer now: the gravel path,

the spade lying by the open
barn, squints of spider floss tightening across
our eyes. Clues, yes, all of these –

but what about this wisp of blood, these
brittle tools? – ghosts
of a weather, your unfathomable skin?

Strange currencies

Because there was no way of seeing
through the jostle of water
nudging our reflection, my mind turned

to other interests: the way
sunflowers stoop to levels that would make
the hair on a dandelion

fizz, and whether all things have shadows apart
from shadows. By the time
the coot had cleared our path – the wake

behind him whispering
to the reeds – an idea began to moil like glass
beneath the stilling surface,

wary of its dimensions, tracing its shape in the faces
wobbling above, weighing
the clouds for some sense of proportion.

Shutters

It was you, pixelating in the flicker
of chapels and shadows,
conjuring a world of swallowtails

with bright uchikake wings,
when a moth settled on the steaming
mirror, Zenning the mist

into delicate scrawl, opening a space
in which I could almost make
my face out, almost not see you.

The ghost grove

And there will be nights
when, lying awake, I will feel the quiet
heat from the moon's skin

and see against a gauze of darkness a you
that isn't you but one woven
from the ghost grove of ancient mulberries

where the mind purls and spins,
hear the mute chaw of silkworms winding
the earth, unmizzling memory.

Tractatus

Because this morning deserves nothing less
than complete idleness,
I will stare into the deep alchemy of my coffee cup

and watch the light filter
down into something gold and fragile and listen
for the ancient fingers

weaving the year's first snowflake. Outside, the wind
is picking up where Spin-
oza left off, while the last leaf left crinkling

to the bough proves
an immortality by ceasing to be. Days are shorter now –
no, we haven't much time.

The things of snow

It came to us from a distance, like a horizon
burning through the forest,
and gathered itself into a shape neither of us

recognised, but knew,
and there it shook while you and I swapped
positions. That's not to say

it resembled snow. It did, but only in the way
that snow resembles
other things. Later, I remembered what it was

and how I'd come
to see it, like waking up and finding that your part
is being played

by someone else. Indeed, 'having a secret isn't
enough'. We also wear
ourselves when naked. Luckily, neither of us

has ever thought
about these things. Let alone the stars. In time,
we'll all begin forgotten.

Working some things through

for Richard Marggraf Turley

In 1739, Jacques de Vaucanson
invented a mechanical
duck that could neither eat

nor fly but could shit
convincingly. Descartes,
who used to swing

a cat by its tail to demon-
strate that it had no soul,
is called the Father

of Modern Philosophy.
'We owe a lot to our pred-
ecessors,' I said to my fluffed-

up friend, the pigeon,
who'd landed next to me,
swooping down from a man-

gled midnightish sky spread
out above us, like the gorge-
ous insides of a god.

The metal clasp

on your leather satchel squeaks
every time you take a step
as though a small bird
were following behind you.
In the coming darkness
the fog grazes at your ankles

like a flock of lost sheep
and you recognise the black one
from tricks the trees used to play
outside your bedroom window.
When the shepherd comes
over the midnight mountains –

his face full of the moon –
you drop your shears to see
what it is he holds
in his outstretched hands –
the silver feathers and the beak,
still quiet in his palms.

The night is like a dinosaur

Sloping by the Museum
of Natural History,
my mind goes out

to all the awkward skeletons
gangling there – their frozen
ribs and roars (

like fossilised parentheses
of a long lost language) –
when suddenly, the whole

sky seems switched on,
like an X-ray of a great being,
whose scattered absence

only the moon's electric
skull and the bare-boned
stars can vertebrate.

Giotto

The morning paper
with its *In Brief,*
about getting to the bottom

after all these years
of the skeleton that they found
in the Duomo crypt,

said that they could tell
who it was from the bad
posture, the over-

extended neck from working
on ceilings, and the pig-
ment metals – man-

ganese and aluminium –
traced in the blood,
sticking to his bones

like plaster. I thought
about that and noticed
that the street around me

was completely empty
and looking up saw
that the sky was a clear

unreal blue – the egg-
white moon was smiling,
telling me I was dreaming.

April morning

A day when the sun is light
without heat
and the shadows lay themselves down

softly. The trees
spend their time trying to remember
their leaves

and the cherry blossom is an empty
thought-bubble above
branch, looking for something to say

to the river,
who has lost himself, daydreaming deer
through the snow.

Flickering out

How far back must one look
to see the junipers whittled
by frost, a winter gloaming in the steel

depth of January skies, before one
recognises a wristwork in the flinging
of shadows, the poise of icicles

pausing along the length of eaves
contemplating mumbletypeg
in the soft slumps of moon-soaked

snow; before one can comprehend
that what they stand for now,
these switchblades of memory,

isn't something slanting
from outside, but a slow sharp
slipping from within.

A suite of bats

Translated from the French of Echen W. Riffier

i

By the time you read this,
I'll have gone to Paris. It's October.
But don't follow me. I've gone crazy.
I've gone to look for my body
in the Seine. My soul in Sacré Coeur.
I'll bring them together over croissants

and *chocolat chaud*. When they separate again,
down cobblestone streets
with broken shutters, I'll watch them
from wrought-iron balconies like a stray note
caught in a stave. But don't follow me,
I'm crazy. If you do, bring me socks to wear

as mittens. Stay away from my coffee.
And the churches. Stay away from the river.
When you get this, read it quickly,
as the words will soon become bats
and fly about the black sky and become far,
far more difficult to read.

ii

You'll see what I mean when you get here.
The sculptures are more alive
than the hedges or trees. More alive
than the man who takes your ticket.
More alive than you, Juan-Christian.
If you walk around the little lawn
where Balzac leans and bulges

and let the gravel crunch under your feet,
and pay no attention to the metaphors
that any of this suggests, you'll begin to see
just what I'm talking about. My hands are cold
and the bushes have whittled themselves down
to a few last red leaves. I wonder whether
you'll notice that – how the bushes are now

completely bare, not a single leaf, or will you
spend your time thinking about the clouds?
About the distant domes? Anyhow, you'll see it
when you get to the fountain behind the château.
To the reflecting pool. That's you looking back,
saying, 'Not all muddy waters are deep.'
It was October. Just before you died.

iii

We'll do this over and over again
till one of us gives. It's like a gavotte.
A bourée. And the music is the thrum
of traffic. A cascade of glass bottles
when the rubbish van comes at 6 a.m.

I overheard someone once refer to the sun
as a glittering disco ball. That was in a hospital
waiting room, and it might not have been
what she said. But there's no doubting
our commitment to learning the right steps,

finding the appropriate shoes. My eyes itch.
And when I prise my fists from my face
I know better than to swat the minuet of fire-
flies floating between us. I used to,
back before I knew that we weren't real.

iv

You'll appreciate, I know, just how
upsetting it was. To look out the back
window of our apartment. At the slanting
roofs down Montmartre. The long
necklaces of lights hanging above the tables
and the wicker chairs. And not recognise
myself in the faces of anyone sitting there,

drinking coffee or having their portraits
sketched. *Moules* is mussels and whatever
the man with the charcoal pencil is drawing
must be from memory. He hasn't looked
at the little girl once. It's nearly October.
I'm with the man sitting alone. He keeps
opening and closing his menu as if rereading

his obituary. He's done with his entrée.
And his main. So am I. And I'm tempted
to call it at two courses. Not wait
for dessert. To tear the sheet off before
my face is finished and hand it to the little girl,
saying, 'Here, sweetheart. Fill in the rest
yourself. With tiny fingerprints. With bats.'

Landscape with coffee and wings

You mustn't read this now. And when
you do, don't tell me. I'd rather not
know. My coat is wet and gulling

to my shoulders like kelp. The sky is fish
and frogs and the people in the café
aren't talking. Their hands are like drift-

wood. On my way here, I passed a woman
pointing to a jar of honey as if to say, 'This is
where I put them. For later.' Anyway, I think

I'm getting smaller. We said we'd meet here,
but we didn't say in which painting. My knees
are blurring. I'm glad you like Brueghel's

Icarus. Why don't we meet there again? – behind
the ploughman and boat, where no one looks
in the water. Where we keep falling.

Philosophy of language

It goes back,
    as all things do,
to that first memory –

    a knife, wide
as my arm,
      and an apple

cézanning beside it –
    something slivering
from a hole and me

    straining to grasp
the pleats pen-
    dulating at the sink,

stuttering, 'Mother,
    is this the thing
that they call fish?'

Sight, unseen

Or take the poet
    thinks he's a dowser
twigging words

    like *sluice* and *sousing*
keeps his ear
    pinned to the rib-

cage of rain-
    drops, palms
for the pulse

    of cacti, shakes
his nib and inks
    a deeper song.

Lacewing

If, as you say, the soul lies
before us, like moons
breaking through the skeleton

leaves of the jacaranda,
a pattern churned and rising
on plumes of dust scuffed

by lost feet – a shape, that is,
that isn't, but one becoming,
one that we can never reach

through reaching – I will
know again the crumpled legs
of the bobbined lacewing,

the strum of the rhombusing
spider, and feel this, our own slow
ghosting, a divination, a home.

Palms

Since neither of us
had ever found ourselves
in such predicament –

the moon's inflection up–
ended, insinuating ice,
and the mist threading

a sequin curtain – we hung
there, reaching beyond
what was reasonable,

even for us, listening
for the snow's fingers
needling somewhere

distant – the leaves
clenching into nothingness
and the sky sifting itself

into what might cradle
in a monkey's palm – a trembling
fistful of stars.